Adulting With Humor Companion Journal

Kim lives in Nebraska with her husband of 36 years, two precious pooches, a litter box-trained bunny, and a duck that quacks her up. She is a mom of two and grandma to three amazing grandchildren. Besides writing, Kim loves to travel, volunteer, and get creative with arts and crafts.

Dedicated to People who:

Love to Laugh
Understand Sarcasm
Like to Journal
Are Fun-Loving
Find Humor in the Ridiculous
Are Frustrated with Adulting

Please leave a review

Thank you for your purchase - it's greatly appreciated.
Reviews are HUGE for an author.
Please leave a review where you purchased the book.

WTF DUCK: Why The Frown? Companion Journal
Written by Kim Wilch
Illustrated by Arti Kukreja

Published by One More Exclamation
Fremont, Nebraska, USA

WTF DUCK: Why The Frown Companion Journal
Paperback ISBN: 979-8-9852463-4-6

WTF DUCK: Why The Frown?
Hardcover ISBN: 979-8-9852463-3-9
Paperback ISBN: 979-8-9852463-2-2

Text © 2022 Kim Wilch. Illustrations © 2022 Arti Kukreja.

All rights reserved. No part of this book may be reproduced or transmitted in any form or by any means, electronic or mechanical, including photocopying, recording, or any info storage and retrieval system, without written permission from the author. Contact: OneMoreExclamation@gmail.com

You quack me up!

Surrounded by idiots.

Ideas I had while pooping:

Were you dropped on your head?

Mistake. Big mistake.

Give me a break.

My favorite drunk story:

Live with intent.

Everyone thought it, I said it.

I don't have my ducks in a row.

I salute you with my middle finger.

Reasons I drink:

Long story short, I'm losing my mind.

Don't be a peckerhead.

Words of wisdom:

I'll pass on your pity party.

Choose joy.

Welcome to the 💩 show.

Notes to self:

No time for drama.

Can't handle the truth? Don't ask me.

Today I'm grateful for:

Do I look like I give a 💩?

Recipe for happiness.

Karma in all its glory.

My doodle space.

Not my circus. Not my monkeys.

Just escaped from the insane asylum.

You're the "she" to my "nanigans".

Dear blogger, just give me the recipe.

Something to laugh about:

Don't do stupid 💩.

Why I need therapy:

The Perfect April Fool's Prank.

Sure, I'd hit that – with a bus.

Expectations let you down everytime.

Thoughts just fly out of my mouth.

Not worth the jail time. Or is it?

Hey, train wreck, this isn't your station.

One glass away from saying what I really think.

So you're a one-upper?

My goals:

My five-year plan:

My ten-year plan:

Advice for idiots.

Ways to mess with people who drive me nuts:

I tested negative for patience.

It's easier to beg for forgiveness than to ask for permission.

I don't give a duck.

Turn that frustration around.

WTF Duck?

Why The Frown

You can only say "WTF" so many times before drinking.

Something to smile about:

Do I look like I care?

My favorite memories:

Be you. If people don't like it, find new people.

My most embarrassing moment.

How about saying it to my face.

I see through your bull💩.

Some bridges need to be burned.

Crazy things my parrot learned to say:

My favorite song lyrics:

Put that in your juice box and suck it.

Let me drink about this.

I wake up tired and go to bed wide awake.

I'm not a morning person.

Is the glass half empty or half full?

Turn that frown upside down.

Thankfully you can't hear my thoughts.

I messed up today.

Shotgun! I'm going crazy.

My inspiration:

Snarky? Hell ya.

Always remember:

People I want to punch in the face:

You can't fix stupid, just numb it with a 2x4.

You're full of 💩

Things that make me smile:

Clever comebacks:

It's a good day for a good day.

Throw sass like confetti.

Sorry, my filter is broken.

Stupid people don't know they're stupid.

What goes around, comes around.

Did I ask for your opinion?

Coffee, because adulting is hard.

A special kind of stupid.

My favorite quotes:

You deserve a high-five!

Hold on, let me overthink this.

Dream. Believe. Achieve.

When life hands you lemons:

Underestimate me, that'll be fun.

Sarcasm: my defense against stupid.

If only common sense was common.

I was left unsupervised.

Inhale tacos. Exhale negativity.

Spoiler Alert! I don't care.

Think outside of the box.

Let the shenanigans begin.

I need an attitude adjustment.

That's a horrible idea. What time?

Mind your own beeswax.

What doesn't kill me makes my drinks stronger.

If only sarcasm burned calories.

Sometimes you have to say "WTF" and move on.

www.ingramcontent.com/pod-product-compliance
Lightning Source LLC
Chambersburg PA
CBHW061405010526
44119CB00011B/266